W9-AQG-336

WHAT'S SO SPECIAL ABOUT PLANET EARTH?

Robert E. Wells

Albert Whitman & Company
Chicago, Illinois

For my brother, Jim, sister-in-law, Susan, and my nephews, Brady and Austin —
special people living on a special planet.

 This book is printed on recycled paper containing 50% post-consumer content.

Library of Congress Cataloging-in-Publication Data

Wells, Robert E.
  What's so special about planet Earth? / Robert E. Wells.
    p. cm.
  ISBN 978-0-8075-8815-4
  1. Earth—Juvenile literature. I. Title.
  QB631.4.W446 2009
  525—dc22 2008056045

The illustration media are pen and acrylic.
Design by Carol Gildar and Robert E. Wells.

For more information about Albert Whitman & Company,
please visit our web site at www.albertwhitman.com.

Also by Robert E. Wells:

Can You Count to a Googol?

Did a Dinosaur Drink This Water?

How Do You Know What Time It Is?

How Do You Lift a Lion?

Is a Blue Whale the Biggest Thing There Is?

Polar Bear, Why Is Your World Melting?

What's Faster Than a Speeding Cheetah?

What's Older Than a Giant Tortoise?

What's Smaller Than a Pygmy Shrew?

PLANET EARTH is not the only planet we know of. But it's a pretty good place for people to live.

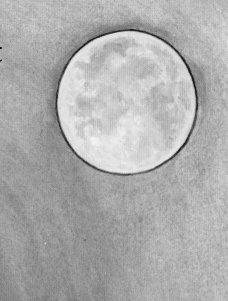

Of course, Earth's weather doesn't always suit us.

Sometimes it's too hot,

or so cold our fingers and toes feel frozen.

Sometimes wild weather

brings hurricanes, tornadoes, and floods.

Suppose you decided you'd like to move to another, more comfortable, planet.

After all, there are 7 other planets to choose from in our solar system.

In the center is the sun, a huge ball of hot gases. With its powerful pull of gravity, the sun holds all the planets in place as they orbit, or travel around it.

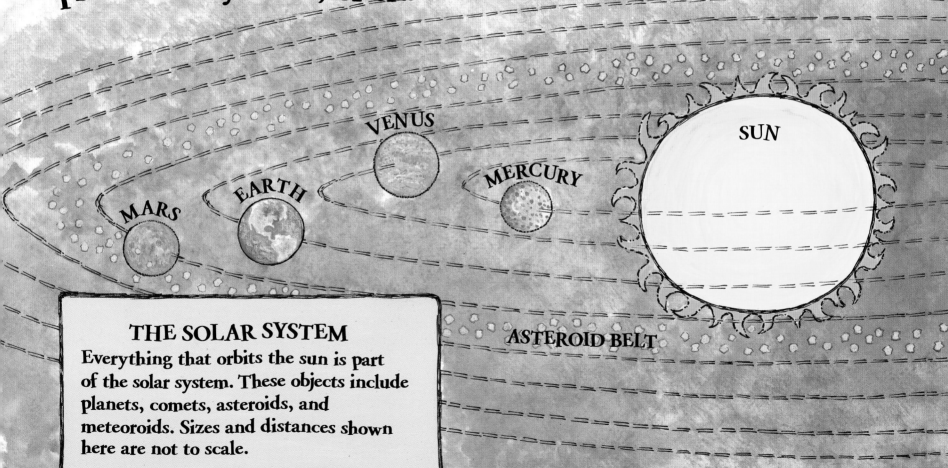

VENUS

MERCURY

SUN

MARS

EARTH

ASTEROID BELT

THE SOLAR SYSTEM
Everything that orbits the sun is part of the solar system. These objects include planets, comets, asteroids, and meteoroids. Sizes and distances shown here are not to scale.

The 8 planets that orbit the sun are Mercury, Venus, Earth, Mars, Jupiter, Saturn, Uranus, and Neptune.

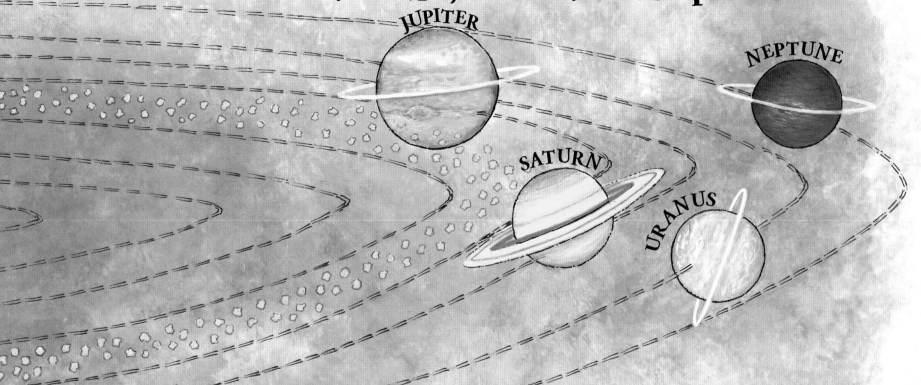

JUPITER

NEPTUNE

SATURN

URANUS

What would it be like to live on another planet, instead of Earth? If you're thinking about moving, you'd want to visit first, to see if the planet is right for you.

Imagine there was a spacecraft fast enough to give you a quick tour of the planets.

First, you'd visit the planets closest to the sun—Mercury, Venus, and Mars. Like Earth, they have solid, rocky surfaces.

Mercury is the closest planet to the sun, and as Mercury has almost no atmosphere, or gases, to protect it,

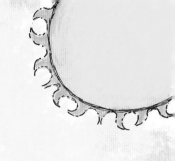

the sun side is a sizzling 800° F. (427° C.), while the dark side is bitterly cold.

Because there's almost no oxygen, no one could breathe on Mercury, even if there were a way to survive in the heat and the cold!

MERCURY
DISTANCE FROM SUN:
36,000,000 MILES

DIAMETER: 3,032 MILES

ORBIT TIME: 88 EARTH-DAYS

MOONS: NONE

We'll try Venus next.

As you approach, you see it's covered with clouds. The surface *isn't* visible!

Is it safe to land?

If the spacecraft pilot lowers you through the clouds, you can see for yourself.

Uh-oh. Your gauges show that the atmosphere is poisonous for people to breathe.

VENUS

DISTANCE
FROM SUN: 67,000,000 MILES

DIAMETER: 7,520 MILES

ORBIT TIME: 225 EARTH-DAYS

MOONS: NONE

It's mostly carbon dioxide, with droplets of sulfuric acid.

And the surface temperature is nearly 900° F. (482° C.)! You couldn't live for a minute here. Get out fast, before you're cooked!

You'll pass through the orbit of Earth, the 3rd planet, on your way to Mars, the 4th planet.

MARS

DISTANCE
FROM SUN: 142,000,000 MILES

DIAMETER: 4,221 MILES

ORBIT TIME: 687 EARTH-DAYS

MOONS: 2

You can land on Mars, but you'll have to put on your spacesuit.

Like Mercury, Mars has almost no oxygen.

You could have fun jumping around on Mars.
The gravity is about 1/3 of Earth's, so you'd be very light.

But Mars's days are usually below
freezing, nights are -100° F. (-73° C.),
and the only known water is frozen
at the poles or under the surface.

People could survive on Mars if they lived in a protective
shelter. But if you like trees, Mars is not for you.

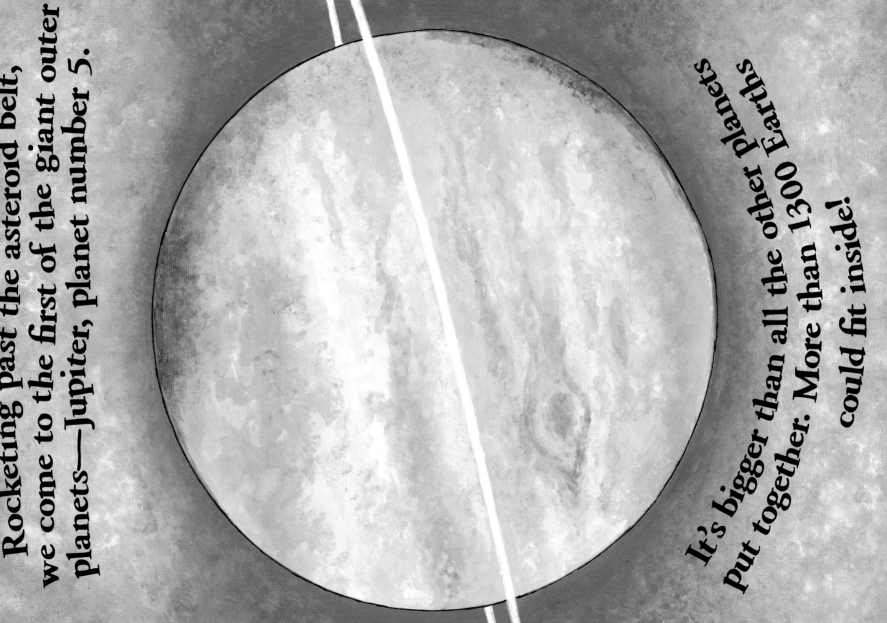

Rocketing past the asteroid belt, we come to the first of the giant outer planets—Jupiter, planet number 5.

It's bigger than all the other planets put together. More than 1300 Earths could fit inside!

But no spaceship could land since Jupiter is made mostly of gas. It's not solid, like Earth.

And talk about storms!

That Great Red Spot, bigger than Earth's diameter, is a giant windstorm that's been raging for 300 years!

JUPITER

DISTANCE
FROM SUN: 483,780,000 MILES

DIAMETER: 88,846 MILES

ORBIT TIME: 12 EARTH-YEARS

MOONS: MORE THAN 60

You can scratch Jupiter off your list of places to live.

Next comes Saturn, the ringed planet. The other outer planets also have rings, but Saturn's rings are the most magnificent.

They're made up of trillions of pieces of ice— from tiny specks to house-sized chunks.

SATURN

DISTANCE
FROM SUN: 886,700,000 MILES

DIAMETER: 74,898 MILES

ORBIT TIME: 29 1/2 EARTH-YEARS

MOONS: 47 SO FAR DISCOVERED

Saturn is cold, stormy, and made mostly of gas. You can't live here.

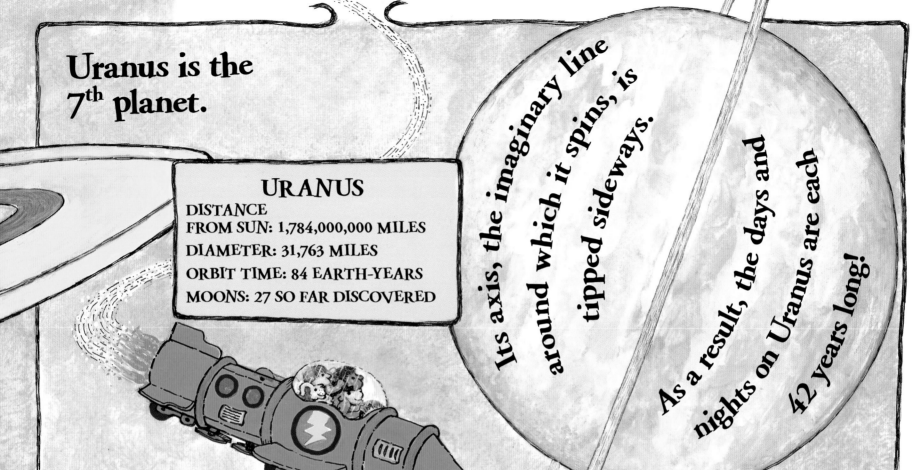

Uranus is the 7th planet.

URANUS

DISTANCE FROM SUN: 1,784,000,000 MILES

DIAMETER: 31,763 MILES

ORBIT TIME: 84 EARTH-YEARS

MOONS: 27 SO FAR DISCOVERED

Its axis, the imaginary line around which it spins, is tipped sideways.

As a result, the days and nights on Uranus are each 42 years long!

Even if Uranus were tipped back up, it would still be a cold, stormy, gas planet, and impossible to live on.

Neptune, the 8th planet, is farthest from the sun, and therefore very cold. Its temperature is -360° F. (-218° C.), and windstorms blow across its surface at 1500 miles per hour!

NEPTUNE

DISTANCE
FROM SUN: 2,795,000,000 MILES

DIAMETER: 30,775 MILES

ORBIT TIME: 165 EARTH-YEARS

MOONS: 13 SO FAR DISCOVERED

Neptune is certainly not a place people can live. It's time to go home—

to our very special planet, Earth.

What makes Earth a just-right place for us?
It's neither too hot nor too cold.
You can breathe—without a spacesuit!
There's plenty of water to drink.

It's good to be back!

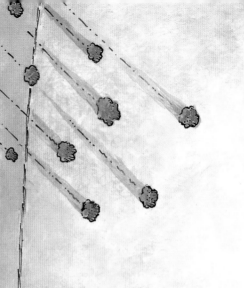

Earth's temperature is right for us because we are the right distance from our sun—about 93 million miles.

Earth's marvelous atmosphere filters out most of the sun's harmful rays . . .

and even protects us from meteors, which usually burn up from air friction.

One-fifth of the atmosphere is oxygen, an ideal proportion of oxygen for Earth's creatures to breathe.

EARTH

DISTANCE
FROM SUN: 93,000,000 MILES

DIAMETER: 7,926 MILES

ORBIT TIME: 365 ¼ DAYS

MOONS: 1

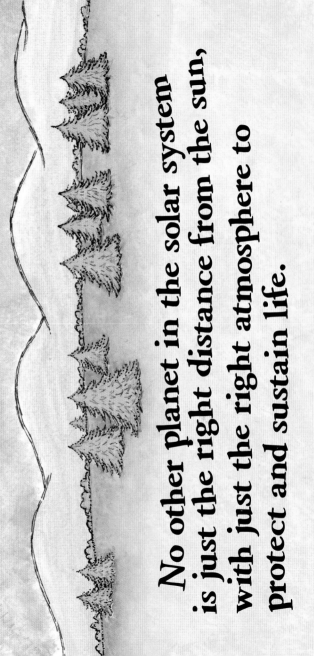

No other planet in the solar system is just the right distance from the sun, with just the right atmosphere to protect and sustain life.

Some of the gases in Earth's atmosphere are called greenhouse gases.

They trap some of the sun's heat,

keeping the air near Earth warmer than it would otherwise be.

This is called the greenhouse effect.

Fresh water to drink makes Earth special.
So does ocean water. About 70 percent of
Earth's surface is covered with ocean.

All living things need water—and no other known
planet has as much water as Earth!

Earth's oceans help life on Earth in different ways.

Millions of people—and other creatures as well—depend on sea life for food.

The oceans also store the sun's heat, and ocean currents circulate the heat to every continent, making the land more comfortable.

Powered by the sun's energy, life-giving fresh water moves all over the world.

1.

The sun's heat evaporates ocean water, turning it into water vapor— leaving the salt behind.

The water vapor rises and forms clouds.

2.

Many of those clouds are blown by the wind over land.

The water from the clouds falls as rain and snow,

3.

creating rivers, streams, and lakes

which give us water for drinking, washing, and growing food.

4.

Much of the water flows back into the oceans and evaporates again,

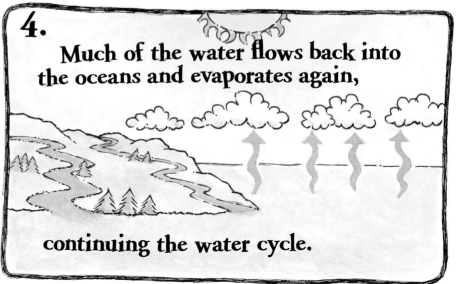

continuing the water cycle.

We have not always taken good care of Earth.

Industrial waste from factories pollutes rivers, streams, and lakes.

Toxic chemicals from landfills seep into underground water storage areas called AQUIFERS.

Sewage and garbage in water can make fish and other animals sick.

Airplanes, ships, motor vehicles, and power plants put huge amounts of carbon dioxide (CO_2) into the air.

All this CO_2 increases the greenhouse effect and makes Earth warmer—too warm for some plants and animals to live.

Growing a vegetable garden can save grocery store trips.

Reusable shopping bags keep plastic bags out of landfills.

Short showers use less water.

By conserving resources and using energy wisely, we can help keep Earth healthy. Here are some things you and your family can do.

Doing these simple things can help, too.

Recycle more

and use less.

Plant trees and bushes—

they absorb pollution from the air.

Put a sweater on

instead of turning up the heat.

Pick up litter

even if it's not yours.

If everyone works together, we can keep Earth a very special place . . .

for ALL of us to live!

How long is a year? Well, it depends on which planet you're on. If you're on Earth, where the days are 24 hours long, it takes 365 1/4 of those 24-hour days to orbit the sun. We call the time it takes Earth to orbit the sun one year.

The farther a planet is from the sun, the longer it takes for it to make one orbit—and the closer it is, the less time it takes. Mercury, the closest planet, has a very short year. If you like birthdays, you'd get to have one every 88 days there. On Mars, farther from the sun than Earth, you'd only have one birthday party every 687 days, or about every two Earth-years. On Neptune, the most distant planet orbiting our sun, you'd never get to have a birthday party at all—it takes 165 of our Earth years to make just one year there!

Our sun is not the only star to have planets orbiting it. Scientists are searching the skies for planets around other distant stars—especially for planets we could possibly visit, and maybe even live on. Over the years, they have discovered that many other stars do have planets orbiting them. But so far, to their disappointment, none appear to be suitable for our kind of life.

Someday, astronomers may discover an Earth-like planet orbiting a distant star, and that would be very exciting news. But even if we did find one, it would be very far away—and therefore very hard to reach.

We don't know for sure if we will ever find another Earth. But one thing we do know: we already have a planet that is just right for us.

If we all work to take care of it, our very special planet, Earth, will be just right for us for a long, long time.